Chronological Children's Bible Gospel Series (Volume 1)

The Birth and Early Life of Jesus Christ

Author:
Swarup Ras

Illustrated by:
Praise punlishing house

Copyright

Chronological Children's Bible Gospel Series Volume 1
The Birth and Early Life of Jesus Christ

ISBN : 978-93-344-0912-3

Scripture Credit
All Scripture quotations are taken from the **World English Bible (Updated Version).**
The World English Bible is in the public domain, and portions are used here to preserve the integrity, accuracy, and beauty of God's Word in full context.

Design & Illustration
Illustrations, Design, and Layout by **Praise Publishing House**
First Edition, 2025

Publisher Information -
Praise Publishing House
praisepublishinghouse.com
connect@praisepublishinghouse.com

This Book,

Chronological Children's Bible
Gospel Series • Volume 1
The Birth and Early Life of
Jesus Christ

Presented to,

____

by

____

On

____

Occasion

____

Dedication

To God Almighty,
the Creator of Heaven and Earth,
and to **Jesus Christ, our Savior and King**
all glory, honor, and praise belong to You forever.

For the Children

May you discover in these pages
that Jesus loves you deeply,
knows your name,
and has written your story in His heart.

For the Parents and Grandparents

Thank you for planting seeds of faith,
for reading God's Word aloud,
and for keeping His light alive in your home.

With Gratitude

To my beloved family and the Praise Publishing House team
your prayers, love, and dedication
have made this work a true offering to God.

May this book shine as a light for generations.
May every Word draw hearts closer to Christ.
May every home be filled with the joy of His presence.

Chapter 1

The Roots of a King

From the very beginning, heaven proclaimed a truth that will never change:

"Jesus Christ is King of kings and Lord of lords."
(Revelation 19:16)

He is the King above every king, the Lord above every ruler, and His kingdom has no end. But unlike earthly kings who suddenly appear in power, God chose a different way to reveal His Son.

This great King was born into a family. He entered our world through a humble stable, into the arms of a young mother, and into a family line carefully prepared across centuries.

Jesus' story as King did not begin in Bethlehem—it began in the heart of God and was written through generations long before His birth.

From Adam to Abraham

Let's go all the way back to the very beginning—to Adam, the very first man. God formed Adam from the dust of the earth and gave him life with His own breath. From Adam came Seth, and after many, many years, a man named Noah was born—the one who built the big boat called the Ark.

After the great flood, Noah's son Shem had children, and so did their children. Many, many generations later, a man named Abraham was born. God made Abraham a beautiful promise:

"Through your family, all the nations of the earth will be blessed." (Genesis 22:18)

That blessing was pointing to Jesus.

From Abraham to David.

Abraham had a son named Isaac, and Isaac had a son named Jacob. One of Jacob's sons was named Judah, and from Judah's family came a shepherd boy named David.

David loved God with all his heart, and one day, he became a mighty king. God told David that someone from his family would be King forever—not just in one country, but over all creation.

That promise also pointed to Jesus.

From King David to Joseph and Mary

After King David, there were many kings and many more generations. Some followed God. Others didn't. But God never broke His promise. He kept weaving His plan through the families of time.

Much later, in a little town called Nazareth, there lived a good man named Joseph. He was a carpenter, and he came from King David's family. Joseph was engaged to a young woman named Mary.

Mary loved God deeply. And one day, an angel would appear to her with the most amazing news.

The Son of Man and the Son of God

Joseph wasn't Jesus' father. God was. Jesus came from heaven.

That's why Jesus is called the Son of God—because He came from the heart of the Father above.

But He's also called the Son of Man—because He was born just like you and me, through a mother, into a family, with cousins, ancestors, and generations before Him.

The Bible says:

"Jesus… was the son (as was supposed) of Joseph… the son of David… the son of Abraham… the son of Noah… the son of Adam, the son of God."

(Luke 3:23–38)

Jesus came to earth to live with us, laugh with us, cry with us, and save us.

He is the King from David's line, the blessing from Abraham's promise, and the Savior of the world from the heart of God.

He is both Son of Man and Son of God.

And His story is just beginning.

Chapter 2

A Promise to a Priest

In the days of King Herod of Judea, there lived a priest named Zechariah, from the family line of Abijah. His wife's name was Elizabeth, and she came from the family of Aaron.

They were both righteous before God, walking blamelessly in all His commandments and ordinances But there was one sadness in their hearts...

"They had no child, because Elizabeth was barren, and they both were well advanced in years." — Luke 1:7

They were old now, and the dream of a child seemed impossible.

One day, Zechariah was chosen by lot—just like drawing names—to go into the Lord's Temple and burn incense. This was a great honor! While the people stood outside praying, Zechariah entered the holy place.

According to the custom of the priest's office, his lot was to enter into the temple of the Lord and burn incense. The whole multitude of the people were praying outside at the hour of incense." — Luke 1:9–10

As the sweet smoke rose into the air, something miraculous happened.
"An angel of the Lord appeared to him, standing on the right side of the altar of incense." — Luke 1:11

Zechariah was startled! He had never seen anything like this.
Zechariah was troubled when he saw him, and fear fell upon him." — Luke 1:12

But the angel spoke gently:
"Don't be afraid, Zechariah, because your request has been heard. Your wife, Elizabeth, will bear you a son, and you shall call his name John." — Luke 1:13

"You will have joy and gladness, and many will rejoice at his birth. For he will be great in the sight of the Lord." — Luke 1:14–15

The angel continued, his voice full of heaven's promise:
"He must drink no wine or strong drink. He will be filled with the Holy Spirit, even from his mother's womb. He will turn many of the children of Israel to the Lord their God." — Luke 1:15–16

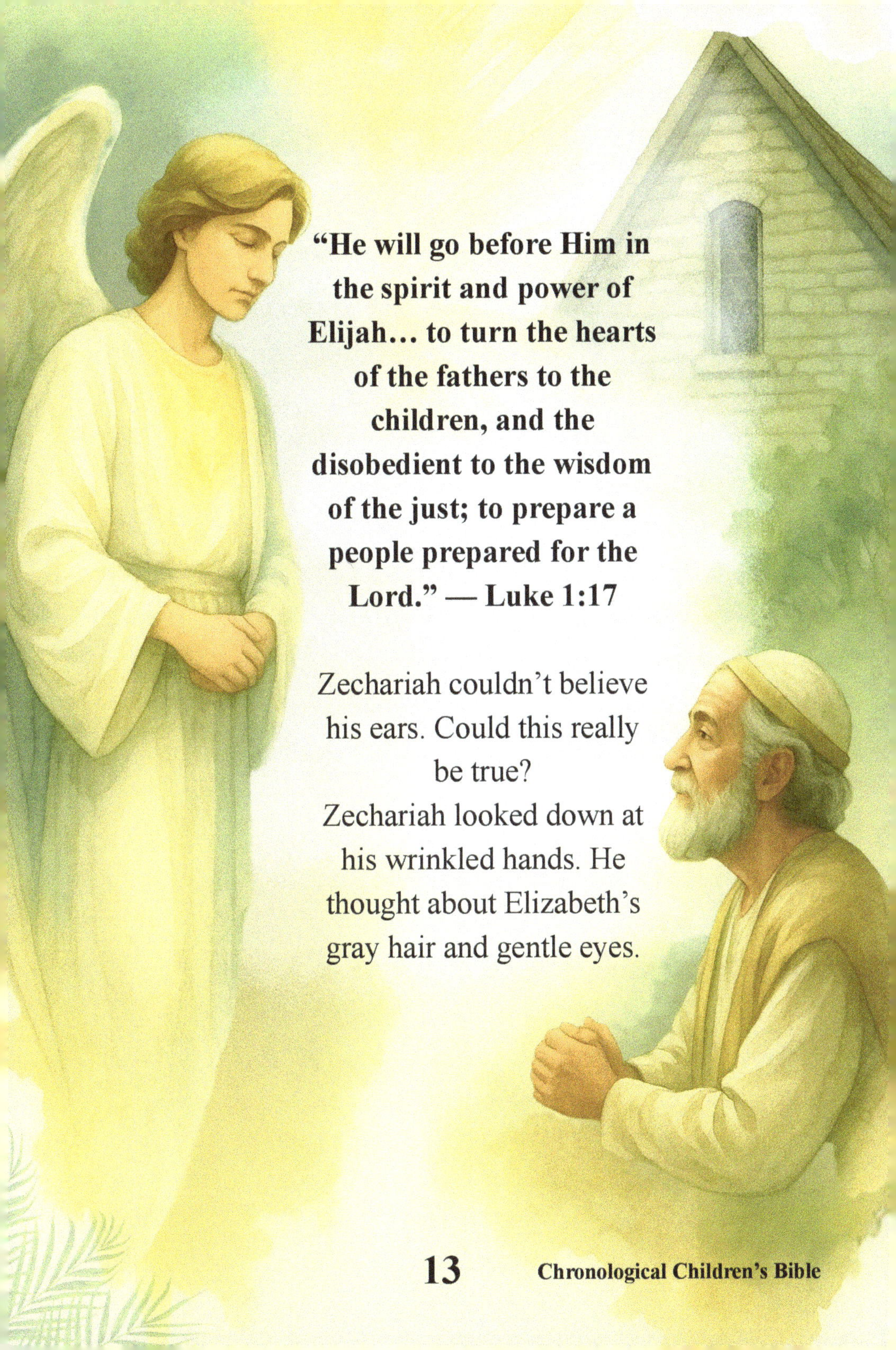

"He will go before Him in the spirit and power of Elijah… to turn the hearts of the fathers to the children, and the disobedient to the wisdom of the just; to prepare a people prepared for the Lord." — Luke 1:17

Zechariah couldn't believe his ears. Could this really be true?
Zechariah looked down at his wrinkled hands. He thought about Elizabeth's gray hair and gentle eyes.

"Zechariah said to the angel, 'How can I be sure of this? For I am an old man, and my wife is well advanced in years.'" — Luke 1:18

The angel stood tall and majestic.
"I am Gabriel, who stands in the presence of God. I was sent to speak to you and to bring you this good news." — Luke 1:19

But then Gabriel's voice became firm:
"Behold, you will be silent and not able to speak until the day that these things happen, because you didn't believe my words, which will be fulfilled in their proper time." — Luke 1:20
Suddenly, Zechariah's voice was gone.
Outside, the people were beginning to wonder.

"The people were waiting for Zechariah, and they marveled that he delayed in the temple." — Luke 1:21

Finally, he came out. But something was different.

"When he came out, he could not speak to them, and they perceived that he had seen a vision in the temple." — Luke 1:22

“He continued making signs to them, and remained mute.” Zechariah finished his time of service and returned home. Not long after, just as the angel said, Elizabeth became pregnant!

“After these days, Elizabeth, his wife, conceived, and she hid herself five months, saying,
‘Thus has the Lord done to me in the days in which He looked at me, to take away my reproach among men.’”
— Luke 1:24–25

She would soon give birth to a baby named John, who would prepare the way for the Savior.

Chapter 3

A Promise to a Girl

It was a quiet day in the small town of Nazareth. In a simple home, a young woman named Mary was going about her chores. She was engaged to a man named Joseph, who was from the family of King David.

Mary didn't know it yet, but heaven was about to visit her.

"Now in the sixth month, the angel Gabriel was sent from God to a city of Galilee named Nazareth, to a virgin pledged to be married to a man whose name was Joseph, of David's house. The virgin's name was Mary." — Luke 1:26-27

Mary looked up—and her heart stopped.

Before her stood a glowing figure. It was Gabriel, the very same angel who had visited Zechariah.

Gabriel smiled and greeted her:

"Rejoice, you highly favored one! The Lord is with you. Blessed are you among women!" — Luke 1:28

Mary froze. She had never heard words like this before. What did this mean? Why was an angel calling her favored?

"But when she saw him, she was greatly troubled at the saying, and considered what kind of greeting this might be." — Luke 1:29

Gabriel's voice was full of peace and promise.

"Don't be afraid, Mary, for you have found favor with God." — Luke 1:30

"Behold, you will conceive in your womb and give birth to a son, and shall name him 'Jesus.'" — Luke 1:31

Gabriel continued with words that made Mary's eyes widen.
"He will be great and will be called the Son of the Most High. The Lord God will give him the throne of his father David, and he will reign over the house of Jacob forever. There will be no end to his Kingdom." — Luke 1:32–33

Mary's heart pounded. A son? A King? The Son of **The Most High?**
She whispered the question in her heart:
"Mary said to the angel, 'How can this be, seeing I am a virgin?'" — Luke 1:34

Gabriel explained gently:
"The Holy Spirit will come on you, and the power of the Most High will overshadow you.
Therefore, also the holy one who is born from you will be called the Son of God." — Luke 1:35
Gabriel gave her a sign, something wonderful:
"Behold, Elizabeth, your relative also has conceived a son in her old age; and this is the sixth month with her who was called barren." — Luke 1:36

Then he smiled and said one of the most beautiful promises in all of scripture:
"For nothing spoken by God is impossible." — Luke 1:37

Mary's eyes filled with tears. Her heart was quiet now. She didn't fully understand—but she trusted.

Mary bowed her head.

She could have said no. She could have doubted or run away. But instead, she offered her whole heart to God.

"Mary said, 'Behold, the servant of the Lord; let it be done to me according to your word.'" — Luke 1:38

Mary's response changed the History

And in that holy moment, the angel Gabriel departed

Mary was left alone in her room—no longer just a girl from Nazareth, but the chosen mother of the Son of God.

Heaven had placed a promise in her womb, and the world would never be the same again.

Chapter 4

A Visit of Joy

Not long after the angel Gabriel left, Mary packed her things and hurried into the hills of Judea.

She had just learned the greatest news of her life—she would be the mother of the Son of God.

But Gabriel had also told her something else:

her cousin Elizabeth, who was very old, was going to have a baby too! Mary needed to see her.

"Mary arose in those days and went into the hill country with haste, into a city of Judah, and entered into the house of Zechariah and greeted Elizabeth." — Luke 1:39-40

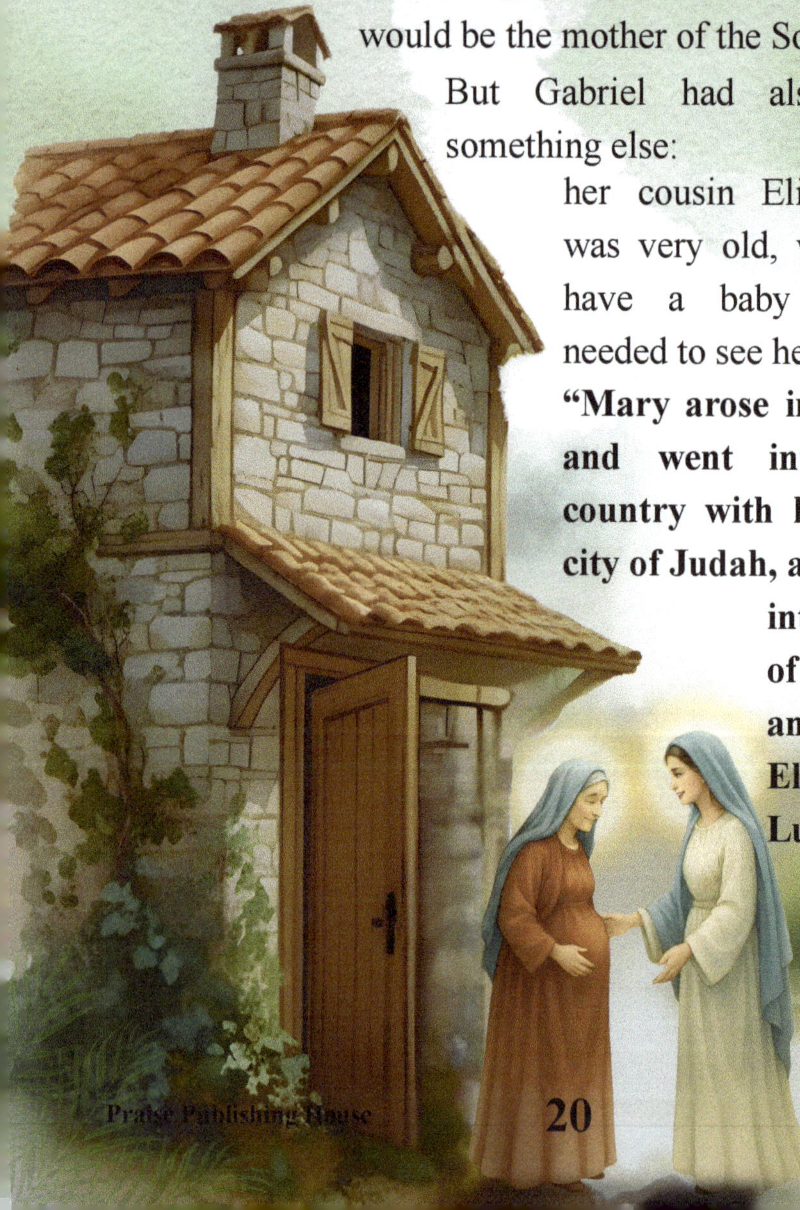

The moment Mary walked through the door and called out her greeting, something incredible happened.

"When Elizabeth heard Mary's greeting, the baby leaped in her womb; and Elizabeth was filled with the Holy Spirit." — Luke 1:41

Elizabeth placed her hands on her belly and began to speak with joy and wonder:

"She called out with a loud voice, and said, 'Blessed are you among women, and blessed is the fruit of your womb!'" — Luke 1:42

"Why am I so favored, that the mother of my Lord should come to me?" — Luke 1:43

Even the baby growing inside Elizabeth—who would become John the Baptist—leaped for joy when Mary came near.

Elizabeth continued, her voice filled with awe:

"For behold, when the voice of your greeting came into my ears, the baby leaped in my womb for joy!" — Luke 1:44

Then she looked into Mary's eyes with deep faith and spoke.

“Blessed is she who believed, for there will be a fulfillment of the things which have been spoken to her from the Lord!” — Luke 1:45

Mary’s heart was full. She had believed the angel. She had said yes to God’s plan.

And now, standing in this room with Elizabeth, she knew—everything the angel said was true. Her soul began to sing.

Mary lifted her voice and began to praise God. Her song has been remembered for thousands of years. It’s called the Magnificat, and it begins like this:

“My soul magnifies the Lord.

My spirit has rejoiced in God my Savior,” — Luke 1:46-47

“For He has looked at the humble state of His servant.

For behold, from now on, all generations will call me blessed.” — Luke 1:48

“For He has looked at the humble state of His servant.

For behold, from now on, all generations will call me blessed.” — Luke 1:48

“For He who is mighty has done great things for me.

Holy is His name.” — Luke 1:49

“His mercy is for generations and generations

on those who fear Him.” — Luke 1:50

Mary’s voice rang with hope and truth:

“He has shown strength with His arm.

He has scattered the proud in the imagination of their hearts." — Luke 1:51

"He has put down princes from their thrones, and has exalted the lowly." — Luke 1:52

"He has filled the hungry with good things. He has sent the rich away empty." — Luke 1:53

"He has given help to Israel, His servant, that He might remember mercy," — Luke 1:54

"as He spoke to our fathers, to Abraham and his offspring forever." — Luke 1:55

Mary stayed with Elizabeth for about three months, until it was almost time for Elizabeth to give birth.
Then, she returned home to Nazareth.

Chapter 5

The Birth of John the Baptist

Elizabeth's house was quiet—but her heart was full.

For so many years, she had waited. And now, the promise had come true. Her baby, the one the angel had told Zechariah about, was ready to be born.

"Now the time that Elizabeth should give birth was fulfilled, and she gave birth to a son." — Luke 1:57

The neighbors came running. Her family gathered. The whole village rejoiced.

"Her neighbors and her relatives heard that the Lord had magnified His mercy toward her, and they rejoiced with her." — Luke 1:58

A miracle had come into their town—a child sent from heaven.

Eight days later, it was time for the special ceremony where the baby would be circumcised and named.

Everyone thought he would be called Zechariah, after his father.

"On the eighth day, they came to circumcise the child; and they would have called him Zechariah, after the name of his father." — Luke 1:59

But Elizabeth shook her head firmly.

"Not so; he will be called John." — Luke 1:60

Everyone was confused! No one in their family had that name.

"They said to her, 'There is no one among your relatives who is called by this name.'" — Luke 1:61

Everyone was confused! No one in their family had that name.

"They said to her, 'There is no one among your relatives who is called by this name.'" — Luke 1:61

They turned to Zechariah, who still hadn't spoken since the day he saw the angel.

Zechariah was handed a writing tablet. With careful strokes, he wrote:

"His name is John." — Luke 1:63

Everyone watched as the words appeared on the wood.

Suddenly, Zechariah opened his mouth—and he could speak!

"His mouth was opened immediately, and his tongue freed, and he spoke, blessing God." — Luke 1:64

Everyone gasped! Whispers filled the room.

"Fear came on all who lived around them, and all these sayings were talked about throughout all the hill country of Judea." — Luke 1:65
"All who heard them laid them up in their hearts, saying, 'What then will this child be?'" — Luke 1:66

And the hand of the Lord was with the child.
Zechariah's heart overflowed. After so many months of silence, his voice returned with praise. The Spirit of God filled him, and he began to speak a prophecy—a powerful song.
"His father Zechariah was filled with the Holy Spirit, and prophesied, saying," — Luke 1:67
"Blessed be the Lord, the God of Israel,
for He has visited and redeemed His people;" — Luke 1:68
"and has raised up a horn of salvation for us in the house of His servant David
(as He spoke by the mouth of His holy prophets who have been from of old)," — Luke 1:69–70
salvation from our enemies, and from the hand of all who hate us;" — Luke 1:71
"to show mercy to our fathers,
to remember His holy covenant," — Luke 1:72
"the oath which He swore to Abraham our father," — Luke 1:73

"to grant to us that we, being delivered out of the hand of our enemies,
would serve Him without fear," — Luke 1:74

Zechariah's voice grew stronger:

"In holiness and righteousness before Him all the days of our life." — Luke 1:75

Then he turned his eyes to the baby in Elizabeth's arms. He spoke softly, but his words echoed with purpose.

"And you, child, will be called a prophet of the Most High;
for you will go before the face of the Lord to prepare His ways," — Luke 1:76

"to give knowledge of salvation to His people by the remission of their sins," — Luke 1:77

because of the tender mercy of our God,
by which the dawn from on high will visit us," — Luke 1:78

"to shine on those who sit in darkness and the shadow of death;
to guide our feet into the way of peace." — Luke 1:79

John grew up strong and full of wonder.

"The child grew, and became strong in spirit, and was in the desert until the day of his public appearance to Israel." — Luke 1:80

His voice would one day thunder in the wilderness. He would call people to turn their hearts back to God. He would point his finger to the Savior and cry out:
"Behold, the Lamb of God!"

But for now…
He was just a baby, cradled in his mother's arms.
A miracle child.
A promised voice.
The one who would prepare the way.

Chapter 6

A Righteous Man's Dream

Mary had returned home to Nazareth. Her heart was full of the angel's words and the promise growing inside her womb. But not everyone understood.

Her fiancé, Joseph, was a kind and honest man. He loved Mary, but now she was expecting a child—and it wasn't his. What should he do?

"Now the birth of Jesus Christ was like this: After his mother, Mary, was engaged to Joseph, before they came together, she was found pregnant by the Holy Spirit." — Matthew 1:18

Joseph was confused… and heartbroken.

"Joseph, her husband, being a righteous man, and not willing to make her a public example, intended to put her away secretly." — Matthew 1:19

He didn't want to shame Mary. He didn't want to hurt her. So quietly, he decided to let her go.

But God had other plans.

That night, Joseph fell asleep… and in his dreams, an angel appeared.

"But when he thought about these things, behold, an angel of the Lord appeared to him in a dream, saying, 'Joseph, son of David, don't be afraid to take to yourself Mary as your wife, for that which is conceived in her is of the Holy Spirit.'" — Matthew 1:20

The angel's voice was calm and full of wonder.
"She shall give birth to a son. You shall call his name Jesus, for it is he who shall save his people from their sins." — Matthew 1:21

Joseph stirred in his sleep, his heart racing. The angel continued:
"Now all this has happened that it might be fulfilled which was spoken by the Lord through the prophet, saying,

'Behold, the virgin shall be with child,
and shall give birth to a son.
They shall call his name Emmanuel,'
which is, being interpreted, 'God with us.'" — Matthew 1:22–23

Joseph awoke with a start.
The morning light poured through the window, but something brighter shone inside his heart.
He knew what to do.

"Joseph arose from his sleep, and did as the angel of the Lord commanded him, and took his wife to himself; and didn't know her sexually until she had given birth to her firstborn son. He named him Jesus." — Matthew 1:24–25

Joseph chose trust.

He chose obedience.

He chose to believe the promise of God—and to raise the Son of God as his own.

Chapter 7

The Journey to Bethlehem and The Birth of Jesus

The wind whispered through the dusty hills of Galilee. People bustled through the streets of Nazareth—packing, preparing, walking. A royal order had been given.

"Now in those days, a decree went out from Caesar Augustus that all the world should be enrolled." — Luke 2:1

"This was the first enrollment made when Quirinius was governor of Syria." — Luke 2:2

Everyone had to travel to their family's hometown to be counted.
And for Joseph, that meant one thing: a long journey to Bethlehem, the city of his ancestor, King David.

"All went to enroll themselves, everyone to his own city. Joseph also went up from Galilee, out of the city of Nazareth, into Judea, to David's city, which is called Bethlehem, because he was of the house and family of David." — Luke 2:3–4

Mary's belly had grown heavy. The time was close. But they had no choice—this journey had to be made.
Joseph walked carefully, making sure the path was safe.

He looked back at Mary again and again. Her face was tired… but peaceful.
"To enroll himself with Mary, who was pledged to be married to him as wife, being pregnant." — Luke 2:5

Day turned to night. The roads were crowded. At last, the small town of Bethlehem came into view—stone buildings, narrow streets, glowing lamps. But it was full of people.

Everyone had come to be counted.
Joseph knocked on door after door, searching for a place to rest.

But every room was taken.
Finally, someone pointed to a quiet place. It wasn't a home. It wasn't a room. But it was warm and sheltered.
A stable.
Joseph cleared a spot among the hay. He helped Mary down gently.
And in that humble place—among animals and straw—heaven touched earth.

"While they were there, the day had come that she should give birth." — Luke 2:6

"She gave birth to her firstborn son. She wrapped him in bands of cloth, and laid him in a feeding trough, because there was no room for them in the inn." — Luke 2:7

Jesus had come.

Not with trumpets, not in a palace, not with a crown…

But as a baby, small and quiet, wrapped in cloth and lying in a manger.

The **King of kings**, born in the most unexpected place.
God had come to be with us—right in the middle of everyday life.
Heaven had come down… and love had taken its first breath.

Chapter 8

Heaven Sings on Earth

Outside of Bethlehem, on a quiet hillside, a group of shepherds watched over their flocks. The stars twinkled above. The sheep dozed peacefully. The only sound was the wind moving gently through the grass.

"There were shepherds in the same country staying in the field, and keeping watch by night over their flock." — Luke 2:8

The shepherds were used to silence. But this night was unlike any other.

Suddenly, the sky split open with light—bright and warm, yet not from the sun or moon.

"Behold, an angel of the Lord stood by them, and the glory of the Lord shone around them, and they were terrified." — Luke 2:9

The shepherds dropped to their knees, shaking.
But the angel's voice was kind.
"Don't be afraid, for behold, I bring you good news of great joy which will be to all the people." — Luke 2:10
"For there is born to you today, in David's city, a Savior, who is Christ the Lord." — Luke 2:11
"This is the sign to you: you will find a baby wrapped in strips of cloth, lying in a feeding trough." — Luke 2:12

Before they could ask another question, the heavens opened even wider.
The sky filled with angels—more than anyone could count.
Their voices rang out in a song the world had never heard before.

"Suddenly, there was with the angel a multitude of the heavenly army praising God, and saying," — Luke 2:13

"Glory to God in the highest,
on earth peace, goodwill toward men." — Luke 2:14
Their song echoed across the hills and into the hearts of the shepherds.
And then, as quickly as they came… the angels were gone.
"When the angels went away from them into the sky…" — Luke 2:15
The silence was deep—but it wasn't empty. It was holy.

The shepherds looked at each other, breathless.

What they had just seen wasn't a dream. It was real. And they knew exactly what they had to do.

"The shepherds said to one another, 'Let's go to Bethlehem, now, and see this thing that has happened, which the Lord has made known to us.'" — Luke 2:15

So they hurried—running down hills, through olive groves, following the stars to find the Savior.

"They came with haste, and found both Mary and Joseph, and the baby was lying in the feeding trough." — Luke 2:16

There He was.

Just like the angel said.

Wrapped in cloth… lying in a manger… and glowing with peace.

The shepherds couldn't stop smiling.

They shared everything they had seen and heard. Everyone in Bethlehem who heard the story was amazed!

"When they saw it, they publicized widely the saying which was spoken to them about this child." — Luke 2:17

"All who heard it wondered at the things which were spoken to them by the shepherds." — Luke 2:18

Mary didn't speak much. She held the baby close and treasured every word in her heart.

"But Mary kept all these sayings, pondering them in her heart." — Luke 2:19

The shepherds returned to their flocks, still full of wonder.

"The shepherds returned, glorifying and praising God for all the things that they had heard and seen, just as it was told them." — Luke 2:20

Chapter 9

Jesus Is Named and Presented at the Temple

Chapter 9

Jesus Is Named and Presented at the Temple

Eight days after the wondrous night when Jesus was born, Mary and Joseph prepared for an important moment. Every baby boy in Israel was to be circumcised and officially given his name.

"When eight days were fulfilled for the circumcision of the child, his name was called Jesus, which was given by the angel before he was conceived in the womb." — Luke 2:21

Mary remembered the angel Gabriel's words when he first visited her: "You shall call his name **Jesus**."

Now, the name was written, spoken, and celebrated.
The name that means "**The Lord Saves**."

Soon, it was time to go to Jerusalem. According to the law of Moses, every firstborn son was to be dedicated to God.

Mary and Joseph traveled from Bethlehem to the grand Temple, carrying their tiny baby.

"When the days of their purification according to the law of Moses were fulfilled, they brought him up to Jerusalem, to present him to the Lord (as it is written in the law of the Lord, 'Every male who opens the womb shall be called holy to the Lord')." — Luke 2:22–23

This was no ordinary baby.
This was the Son of God being presented in His Father's house.

Mary and Joseph weren't wealthy. The law said they could bring a lamb for the offering, but if they couldn't afford it, they could bring two birds instead.
So they brought two small doves, a humble but heartfelt gift to God.

"And to offer a sacrifice according to that which is said in the law of the Lord, 'A pair of turtledoves, or two young pigeons.'" — Luke 2:24

Mary kissed the baby's forehead. She whispered a prayer, knowing that this little child would one day give Himself for the whole world.

Chapter 10

Simeon and Anna Meet the Savior

The Temple was busy—full of people, prayers, and priests. But among the crowds that day, one man stood waiting. His name was Simeon.

He was old and full of wisdom. He loved God with all his heart, and he longed for the coming of the Messiah—the one who would save Israel.

"Behold, there was a man in Jerusalem whose name was Simeon. This man was righteous and devout, looking for the consolation of Israel, and the Holy Spirit was on him." — Luke 2:25

Simeon wasn't just hoping—he had a promise.

"It had been revealed to him by the Holy Spirit that he should not see death before he had seen the Lord's Christ." — Luke 2:26

That morning, the Spirit whispered to his heart: "Go to the Temple."

And he did.

At the very same time, Mary and Joseph entered with baby Jesus.

Simeon's heart leapt. The moment he saw the child, he knew—this was Him. The Savior. The Light. The Promise.

Simeon stepped forward, his hands trembling—not with fear, but joy.

Mary looked at Joseph. Joseph nodded.

She placed baby Jesus into Simeon's arms.

Simeon looked into the baby's face and began to speak words filled with heaven:

"Then he received him into his arms, and blessed God, and said," — Luke 2:28

"Now you are releasing your servant, Master, according to your word, in peace;" — Luke 2:29

"For my eyes have seen your salvation, which you have prepared before the face of all peoples;" — Luke 2:30–31

"A light for revelation to the Gentiles, and the glory of your people Israel." — Luke 2:32

Mary and Joseph stood amazed at what was being said.

"Joseph and his mother were marveling at the things which were spoken concerning him." — Luke 2:33

Then Simeon looked into Mary's eyes. His face was full of love—but also a quiet sadness.

"Simeon blessed them, and said to Mary, his mother, 'Behold, this child is set for the falling and the rising of many in Israel, and for a sign which is spoken against.'" — Luke 2:34

"Yes, a sword will pierce through your own soul,
that the thoughts of many hearts may be revealed." — Luke 2:35

Mary held Jesus a little closer. Her eyes glistened, but her heart remained calm. Just then, someone else stepped near...

Chapter 11

The Faithful Prophetess

While Simeon was still holding baby Jesus and speaking his blessing, someone else stepped into the light. Her name was Anna.

She was very old—eighty-four years old—but her eyes sparkled like someone full of life and love. She was a prophetess, a woman who listened to God and spoke His truth.

"There was one Anna, a prophetess, the daughter of Phanuel, of the tribe of Asher (she was of a great age, having lived with a husband seven years from her virginity, and she had been a widow for about eighty-four years)," — Luke 2:36-37

Anna had lived in the temple for many years. Day after day, night after night, she prayed. She worshiped. She fasted. She waited.

"She didn't depart from the temple, worshiping with fasting and petitions night and day." — Luke 2:37

That day, as Simeon praised God and blessed the family,
Anna saw them.
Her heart leapt.
Her waiting was over.

"Coming up at that very hour, she gave thanks to the Lord, and spoke of him to all those who were looking for redemption in Jerusalem." — Luke 2:38

She didn't need to be told. She knew.
This baby—this small child in Mary's arms—was the one she had been waiting for.

She praised God with joy, and told everyone she could:
"The Savior is here! The Redeemer has come!"

And even though her name appears in just a few verses, her story lives forever—because she was ready when the moment came.

Chapter 12

Visitors from Afar

Far from Bethlehem, across deserts and rivers, mountains and valleys, lived **Wise men** who studied the stars. They were called **Magi**, and they came from the East.

One night, they saw something unusual—a bright star rising in the sky. It wasn't like any other star they had ever seen. It felt like a message from heaven.

They packed their gifts and began their long journey. The star was leading them to a King.

"Now when Jesus was born in Bethlehem of Judea in the days of King Herod, behold, wise men from the east came to Jerusalem, saying, 'Where is he who is born King of the Jews? For we saw his star in the east, and have come to worship him.'" — Matthew 2:1–2

The wise men arrived in Jerusalem, the capital city. They expected people would already know where the new King was.

But the city was confused.

"When King Herod heard it, he was troubled, and all Jerusalem with him." — Matthew 2:3

King Herod was not happy. He didn't want another king—especially one sent by God.

"Gathering together all the chief priests and scribes of the people, he asked them where the Christ would be born." — Matthew 2:4

The priests searched the scriptures and found the answer.

"They said to him, 'In Bethlehem of Judea, for this is written through the prophet,'" — Matthew 2:5

"'You Bethlehem, land of Judah, are in no way least among the princes of Judah;

for out of you shall come a governor who shall shepherd my people, Israel.'" — Matthew 2:6

Herod pretended to be kind.

"Then Herod secretly called the wise men, and learned from them exactly what time the star appeared." — Matthew 2:7

"He sent them to Bethlehem, and said, 'Go and search diligently for the young child. When you have found him, bring me word, so that I also may come and worship him.'" — Matthew 2:8

But Herod wasn't being honest.
The wise men thanked him and set out again—following the star.
"They, having heard the king, went their way; and behold, the star, which they saw in the east, went before them until it came and stood over where the young child was." — Matthew 2:9

The star had found its place.
And so had they.
"When they saw the star, they rejoiced with exceedingly great joy." — Matthew 2:10

They entered the house—and there He was.

Jesus.

No longer a newborn in a manger, but a small child, held in His mother's arms.
The wise men bowed low, their hearts full of awe.
"They came into the house and saw the young child with Mary, his mother, and they fell down and worshiped him." — Matthew 2:11

Then the Magi opened their treasures.

"Opening their treasures, they offered to him gifts: Gold, Frankincense, and Myrrh." — Matthew 2:11

Each gift was special.

- Gold for a King.
- Frankincense for the Son of God.
- Myrrh, a reminder that this child would one day suffer and save the world.

But their journey wasn't over.

That night, God spoke to them in a dream.

"Being warned in a dream not to return to Herod, they went back to their own country another way." — Matthew 2:12

They left quietly, hearts changed forever by the child they had found.

Chapter 13

A Midnight Escape

That night, the stars shone quietly over Bethlehem.

Mary had wrapped Jesus in a warm blanket. Joseph sat nearby, his tools folded neatly in the corner. The wise men had gone, and the town was falling asleep.

But in the deep silence, heaven spoke again.

Now, when they had departed, behold, an angel of the Lord appeared to Joseph in a dream, saying,
'Arise and take the young child and his mother, and flee into Egypt, and stay there until I tell you,
for Herod will seek the young child to destroy him.'" — Matthew 2:13

Joseph sat up, heart racing. Another dream—another message from God.

He didn't hesitate.

Without wasting a moment, Joseph rose and woke Mary. They wrapped Jesus carefully, gathered what little they had, and stepped into the darkness.

The wind was cool. The night was quiet. But God's presence went before them.

"He arose and took the young child and his mother by night, and departed into Egypt." — Matthew 2:14

Step by step, they left behind Bethlehem and followed the road toward safety—away from danger, away from Herod.

They stayed in Egypt for some time—safe and hidden under God's protection.

"And was there until the death of Herod,
that it might be fulfilled which was spoken by the Lord through the prophet, saying,
'Out of Egypt I called my son.'" — Matthew 2:15

Long ago, God had called the people of Israel out of Egypt through Moses.

Now, He was calling His Son out of Egypt too—Jesus, the Savior.

Even as a little child, God's plan was being fulfilled step by step.

No king, no danger, and no darkness could stop what God had promised.

Chapter 14

A Cry in Ramah

Back in Jerusalem, King Herod waited.

He had told the wise men to return with news of the child's location—but they never came.

"Then Herod, when he saw that he was mocked by the wise men, was exceedingly angry." — Matthew 2:16

His heart burned with jealousy and fear. He didn't want another king.

So he did something terrible.

"He sent out, and killed all the male children who were in Bethlehem and in all the surrounding countryside, from two years old and under, according to the exact time which he had learned from the wise men." — Matthew 2:16

It was a dark and heartbreaking day.

The cries of the mothers rose through the streets. The sound reached heaven.

"Then that which was spoken by Jeremiah the prophet was fulfilled, saying," — Matthew 2:17

"A voice was heard in Ramah,
lamentation, weeping, and great mourning,
Rachel weeping for her children;
she wouldn't be comforted,
because they are no more." — Matthew 2:18

It was a prophecy—one spoken long ago. And now, it had come true.

But even in this darkness, God was at work.

He had sent Jesus away in time. The Rescuer was still alive. The Savior was safe.

And one day, He would wipe away every tear.

Chapter 15

A New Home in Nazareth

In the land of Egypt, far from Bethlehem, Joseph, Mary, and little Jesus lived quietly. No one knew who they were. But heaven had not forgotten them.

One night, the angel returned—this time not with a warning, but with peace.

"But when Herod was dead, behold, an angel of the Lord appeared in a dream to Joseph in Egypt, saying,"
— Matthew 2:19

"'Arise and take the young child and his mother, and go into the land of Israel,
for those who sought the young child's life are dead.'"
— Matthew 2:20

Joseph rose with hope. The danger was gone. It was time to go home.

They journeyed back into the land of Israel, step by dusty step.

But Joseph heard that Archelaus, Herod's son, was now ruling in Judea. Joseph became afraid—and once again, God spoke to him in a dream.

“He arose and took the young child and his mother, and came into the land of Israel.
But when he heard that Archelaus was reigning over Judea in the place of his father, Herod,
he was afraid to go there.” — Matthew 2:21–22

“Being warned in a dream, he withdrew into the region of Galilee, and came and lived in a city called Nazareth…” — Matthew 2:22–23

And there, in the quiet town of Nazareth, Jesus grew.

“…that it might be fulfilled which was spoken through the prophets:
He will be called a Nazarene.’” — Matthew 2:23

Chapter 16

Jesus Grows in Wisdom

Time passed quietly in Nazareth.

No angels appeared. No stars filled the sky. No visitors came from far away.

But something beautiful was happening—Jesus was growing.

He laughed. He played. He helped Joseph in the carpenter's shop. He watched Mary knead bread. He studied the scriptures and learned to pray.
And God's hand was on Him.
"The child was growing and was becoming strong in spirit,
being filled with wisdom,
and the grace of God was upon him." — Luke 2:40

He was no longer just the baby in the manger.
He was now a boy—full of joy, full of questions, full of God's Spirit.

Chapter 17

The Boy in the Temple

Every year, Joseph and Mary made a special journey from Nazareth to Jerusalem for the Feast of the Passover.

It was a time to remember how God had rescued His people long ago. It was a time of songs, prayers, and celebration.

When Jesus was twelve years old, He came with them.

"His parents went every year to Jerusalem at the feast of the Passover.

When he was twelve years old, they went up to Jerusalem according to the custom of the feast." — Luke 2:41–42

It was a beautiful and busy time.

But what happened next… surprised everyone.

When the festival was over, Joseph and Mary packed up to return to Nazareth.
They thought Jesus was walking with the group—maybe with cousins or friends.
But when evening came… they couldn't find Him.
"When they had fulfilled the days, as they were returning,
the boy Jesus stayed behind in Jerusalem.
Joseph and his mother didn't know it." — Luke 2:43

"But supposing him to be in the company,
they went a day's journey,
and they looked for him among their relatives and acquaintances." — Luke 2:44

They searched everywhere. On the roads. In the homes of friends. Among other travelers.
But He wasn't there.
So they turned around and went back to Jerusalem.
"When they didn't find him, they returned to Jerusalem, looking for him." — Luke 2:45

They searched for three days.

Finally, they entered the temple… and found Him.

"After three days, they found him in the temple, sitting in the middle of the teachers, both listening to them and asking them questions." — Luke 2:46

The teachers were amazed.

"All who heard him were amazed at his understanding and his answers." — Luke 2:47

Mary hurried to Jesus.

"When they saw him, they were astonished, and his mother said to him, 'Son, why have you treated us this way? Behold, your father and I were anxiously looking for you.'" — Luke 2:48

Jesus turned to her and spoke gently—yet with great truth:

"He said to them,
'Why were you looking for me?
Didn't you know that I must be in my Father's house?" — Luke 2:49

In the KJV Bible, the translation says, **"And he said unto them, How is it that ye sought me?**
Wist ye not that I must be about my Father's business?"

Mary didn't fully understand what He meant…

"They didn't understand the saying which he spoke to them." — Luke 2:50

But even so, Jesus didn't stay behind again.

He returned with them to Nazareth—obedient, humble, and full of grace.

"And he went down with them, and came to Nazareth.
He was subject to them, and his mother kept all these sayings in her heart." — Luke 2:51

"And Jesus increased in wisdom and stature,
and in favor with God and men." — Luke 2:52

He was no longer just Mary's little boy. He was beginning to grow into the Savior the world had been waiting for. He was on **Father's business.**

A Note of Thanks

Dear Reader,
Thank you for reading Chronological Children's Bible · Gospel Series · Volume 1 – The Birth and Early Life of Jesus Christ.

Each page was prayerfully designed with complete Bible Scriptures blended with story and illustration, so that children and families can read the true and living Word of God as it was written — timeless, powerful, and life-giving.

If this book has blessed your heart, we warmly invite you to share your honest review on Amazon, Goodreads, Ingram Spark, or praisepublishinghouse.com. Your words help others discover the joy of engaging with Scripture and encourage us to keep creating Christ-centered books.

Praise Publishing House exists to make "*Bible Engagement Through Creativity*" a reality for every generation — turning creativity into worship through illustrated devotionals, story Bibles, and activity books that draw hearts closer to Jesus.

Our Vision: To inspire hearts to know, love, and live God's Word.

Our Mission: To bring Scripture to life through creative storytelling, art, and devotion that strengthen families and glorify God.

Coming Soon:

1) Unlocking Proverbs Adventures Of Ella And Sam Part 1
(Fiction Story for young adults on the book of Proverbs covering all 31 chapters.)

2) 40 Days With Psalms.
An Immersive Word Search puzzle book for Seniors.

3) Grow Up with Jesus: The Christmas Story And Beyond
Chronological Bible in Coloring Book format. (Revised Edition).

Available title on Amazon

Finding Peace, Comfort, and Strength Through Psalms

A Coloring Devotional book covering Psalm 23, 91, 121, and 27

With gratitude and blessings,
The Praise Publishing House Family
praisepublishinghouse.com

www.ingramcontent.com/pod-product-compliance
Ingram Content Group UK Ltd.
Pitfield, Milton Keynes, MK11 3LW, UK
UKHW061304190726
13845UKWH00035B/1257

9 789334 409123